THE FIRST CLASS FORMULA

ALL THE SECRETS YOU SHOULD KNOW TO SUCCEED AT UNIVERSITY

ROBERT HANSON • JACOB BANFIELD • DANIEL CLARK

THE FIRST CLASS FORMULA Copyright © 2012 by Robert Hanson, Jacob Banfield and Daniel Clark. All rights reserved.

No part of this publication may be used or reproduced in any manner whatsoever without written permission except in the case of brief quotations embodied in critical articles and reviews.

Limit of Liability/Disclaimer of Warranty: While the publisher and authors have used there best efforts in preparing this book, they make no representation or warranties with respect to the accuracy of completeness of the contents of this book and specifically disclaim any implied warranties of merchantability or fitness for a particular purpose. The advice and strategies contained herein may not be suitable for your situation. Neither the publisher or author shall be liable for any loss of profit, lack of attainment or any other commercial damages, including but not limited to special, incidental, consequential, or other damages.

The Zen student balances their studies with their social life. They know that the journey is just as important as the destination.

Contents

Preface	6
How to Use This Book	9
Our Story and Why You Need This Book	12
The Art of Studying	17
How to Write the Perfect Essay	35
How to Ace the Exams	59
The Lifestyle	79
The Winning Mentality	101
The Last Chapter	111
Bonus Material	113
The Ten Commandments of Referencing	115
Recipes	119
Recommended Reading	125
Glossary	129
Acknowledgements	137
A Message From the Authors	139

Preface

There is a formula for success at university, you can achieve a first class degree and have a great time. We will share this formula with you, but it is up to you to use it. Right now, graduation is probably the last thing on your mind and that is a good thing. Do not listen to what other people say. It will not come round sooner than you think. Not if you experience every moment fully.

If you have done what it takes and achieved the results you needed to get to university, well done. People underestimate the distractions A-level students face when at college. We forget that during the transition from the first to the second year of college the average student turns eighteen. They can now drive their first car, legally drink alcohol and are discovering sex. Academic learning is definitely not their priority. So, now you've arrived at university, the real fun begins.

It's true. Hindsight is a wonderful thing. It is only after you've done something you realise whether or not you did it right, but more importantly, how you did what you did. Upon graduation we looked back on our university career and thought that we could not have done it any better. Those three years were the best of our lives so far and we would not change a thing. Quite simply we wanted other people to be able to say the same thing when they graduated too.

The truth is though, we realised with more strategy, getting our first class degrees should have been easier. If only we had developed the formula sooner. But that is just it we didn't, but you can. Most people think you have to study non-stop to get a first class degree. That is not true, you have to study smart. You can balance your academic work with an incredible social life. You don't have to choose between one or the other. We believe you can have the best of both worlds.

To really lead an incredible life at university, studying is just part of the story. The student with the highest IQ doesn't always get the best marks. If you understand how to apply the formula, not only will you achieve a first class degree but you will also have a first class time doing it. The academic system is not perfect, so it is up to you to learn how to beat the system. In this book we are giving you the inside track and the hidden truths in your path to becoming the Zen student.

Getting a first class degree at university is not always an easy journey, but it is definitely one worth taking. We hope you enjoy reading this book as much as we enjoyed writing it and reliving our university experience.

How to Use This Book

This book is your blueprint to studying at university on your own terms. The steps and insights contained within can be used to gain incredible results. Here are the skills you will use to get a first class degree:

The Art of Studying

Find out the key differences between studying at university compared to college. Follow three easy steps to find the best way of studying for you. Learn these now and it will put you in the best position to handle every aspect of your course. Have more free time and double your productivity. This chapter will start you on the right track.

How to Write the Perfect Essay

We provide you with a strategy to handle any essay. From the basics through to high-level academic techniques that you can implement instantly. These tips will make your essay stand out from the crowd. Remember, you cannot write the perfect essay, but you can get pretty close.

How to Ace the Exams

There are two phases to acing your exams. Preparation and technique. We show you how to really test yourself and then what to do about it. Network your way to great results. Uncover your own exam ritual and learn the unknown methods that really gain high marks.

The Lifestyle

Read this chapter to become the person other students come to for advice. Start university with the wisdom to make the right decisions. Find your house spirit. Learn to balance every aspect of your experience without breaking a sweat.

The Winning Mentality

The final piece of the puzzle. Discover the mindset that exists within you to put the formula into action. Create your own personal brand and learn to use failure to your advantage.

Our Story and Why You Need This Book

Robert Hanson:

Back in college, I never had any intentions of heading to university. No more education I thought. Three years later, after graduating with the best degree on my course, I guess I thought wrong. Completing university was the best thing I ever did. The experience was invaluable. I learned so much, not just academically but about life too. From the moment I attended that first lecture to collecting my scroll at graduation. Whether I knew it or not, I was always learning, I still am. It was an incredible feeling finding out I received a first. It proved to me that preparation and hard work does pay off. But looking back I realised it was not just hard work, it was also working smart.

I wrote this book because I believe there is a first class formula, a method to achieving a first class degree and having a great experience. It is a desire and lifestyle, you have to want it and live it. I want you to use what we say and fulfil your potential. My aim is solely to show you the way, how it can be done, to give you the knowledge and wisdom to have the greatest time of your life and walk away with the gold.

Jacob Banfield:

This was the moment of truth. It was time to discover if all of our hard work had paid off. I was at Wimbledon standing in the middle of centre court, literally. I was working there during the Tennis Championships. The stadium was empty, which was probably a good thing. My heart was racing.... "You have been awarded a First Class Bachelor of Science Degree with Honours". I can tell you, there is no feeling quite like it. To put your heart and soul into something and achieve what you set out to accomplish. It felt like I had just lifted the trophy.

For me, university was a place of self-discovery. I got my heart broken for the first time, I performed on stage in front of 200 people and I made lifelong friends. During my first two years at university, I coasted. It was only at the beginning of the third year that I realised I had a chance of getting a first. So, I made it my mission. I want to give you the information that I never had. Not so you forget about studying, but so you can understand that every aspect of university is integral to your experience. It will be a journey. I hope you discover who you are, learn something along the way and share your experience. That will be truly first class.

Daniel Clark:

I remember results day clearly. The defining moment had come. I looked down at my phone, my head could not process the information on the screen. I became delusional and frantically tried to understand what degree class I had been awarded. It took a while to settle in. I had fallen short. I had been awarded the best 2.1 in the country. Mathematically I could not have been closer to getting a first. Only 'half a mark' in one of my exam papers would have made all the difference. Honestly, not half a per cent, only half a mark. No more than a spelling mistake.

Over the next few months, the university sent me on a rollercoaster ride. I was provisionally awarded a 'virtual' half a mark and stood there on graduation day celebrating a first class degree with friends and family. A few weeks later, I received terrible news. New regulations meant that this decision had been blocked.

As I write these words, those horrific few months replay in my head. I would not wish it on anyone. That is why I am writing this book. I want to make sure you go out and get your half a mark. It will not be given to you. You have to earn it.

To all the students who missed by half a mark.

The Art of Studying

I hated every minute of training, but I said. Don't quit. Suffer now and live the rest of your life as a champion.
- MUHAMMED ALI

Learning never exhausts the mind.
- LEONARDO DA VINCI

Mission: This chapter lays out three easy steps to discover the best way of studying for you. With this knowledge you will be able to manage your time effectively and double your productivity. Revise, refresh or research, it is all here.

- THE IMPORTANCE OF - STUDYING

Those who take shortcuts, get cut short.
- REVEREND RUN

To most people, studying is a 'means to an end' activity that has to be done whether you like it or not. It can be an arduous experience. The truth is there are no shortcuts, only ways to make the road smoother.

The art of studying should not be about processing and storing information, computers do that, not people. The one thing to remember is that studying for the sake of studying is like running on a treadmill, you are running but not actually getting anywhere. To be effective when studying, you must know what you are trying to achieve.

Studying at university is different to college, it becomes a way of life. It can be whatever you want it to be. Learn the art of studying using the three steps in this chapter. This philosophy will help you to attain a first class degree and serve you throughout life.

Step I
- ORGANISATION -

Motion creates emotion.
- JIM YOUNG, BOILER ROOM

To begin a task you must first have the tools in place to complete it. In the book 'Do It Tomorrow', the author Mark Forster suggests that by saying to yourself, "I'm not really going to start work, I'm just going to get the equipment out" you short circuit the urge to procrastinate. So by having the necessary tools out, you trick yourself into studying.

The System

You need to have a system. This ensures you are ready for action. It engineers the feeling that you are ready to study, to learn and to deal with whatever your lecturer throws at you. You can rely on your system and it will be there to support you when you need it. This preparation behind the scenes maximises the benefits of attending lectures, taking notes and learning your subject.

Okay, so what is the system? Well the good news is you don't have to pay us £19.99 for the next twelve months or scroll down to find out about this miracle product. The system is simply a method of organising your work, so you can access it quickly and easily in the future.

Each year, your university course will be separated into a number of modules or subjects. Having just one workbook for all of these will make things messy, like an 'It's complicated' relationship on Facebook. By creating a system, essentially you are breaking your work down into manageable volumes, whereby it becomes easy to access any piece of work quickly. The benefits of this method are that it is easier to find material for essays and to revise for exams.

Insight – The Method of Loci: One of the hidden benefits of creating an organised system is that you will be able to mentally access your notes in an exam. Unconsciously, you will create a mind palace, a collection of important facts and associations relevant to the subject.

Components

- 1 x Lined workbook or notepad per subject
- 1 x Folder per subject to file the notes away in order as the course progresses
- 1 x Holepunch
- Plastic wallets to store journal articles and other required reading

Now your choice of paper, whether it is Tesco Value, a Pukka Pad or those artisan notebooks they sell in Waterstones, is completely up to you. One thing to bear in mind is that your system should run like a good business, by keeping costs down while upping productivity.

Here is the sticking point. It is easy to get lost in the system. It should only exist to streamline your activities and allow you to get the maximum benefit from the university experience. It is a support mechanism and it should not be running you. Do not just attend the lectures, file something away and think that your work is done. It is far too easy to concentrate on maintaining a perfectly organised folder, when the truth of the matter is that you do not really understand the value of what is inside.

Insight - Function over Fashion: Forget colour coding and fancy title pages unless it actually helps productivity. Do not waste time dressing up your system.

You will find the best way to organise your work is through experimentation. But this should not be the end goal. The end goal should be the acquisition of knowledge. With knowledge comes power, the power to succeed. A well-organised system will pay dividends at revision time.

Step II
- HOW TO STUDY -

There are two types of student, those who say they are studying and those that actually do it.

There is a technique to studying, and everybody's is different. It becomes easier to study by understanding the process that works best for you.

To pass your course you must fulfil the framework set out by your department, whether that is writing essays, sittings exams, giving presentations or carrying out experiments. This is the bureaucracy, this is the only way you will pass, by jumping through their hoops. You must find out the best method of studying for yourself, and the following considerations will help you to achieve this.

The Google Attitude

The Google attitude is the mindset to understand something beyond your depth of knowledge. Everything is just a Google search away. If you read a word and do not know what it means, Google it. Use the power of the Internet to find any answer. Adopt this attitude, not only in your studies but also in life. It will serve you well. At the end of each chapter we have set a challenge that requires the Google attitude.

Environment

The environment you choose to study in will directly affect the outcome of your work. Wherever this may be, it must feel like a place to study. There are a variety of places that may work for you and it does not have to be restricted to just one. It needs to be a place that allows you to get in the right state of mind, a place where you can fully immerse yourself and eliminate distractions.

▶Home

Take studying at home for example. Some people enjoy the peace and quiet of their home. Without getting spiritual, you are surrounded by familiar objects that calm your mind and allow you to fully concentrate on the task at hand. You have no travel time, can begin as soon as you want and should hunger strike the kitchen is right next door.

▶Library

The library can be a great place to study. After all it is the epicentre of knowledge. Here you can work in an area specifically designed for researching, reading and learning. It is a quiet place without many distractions. The beauty of this space is that you are surrounded by like-minded students all working on their own individual subjects. This creates a nice synergy, which reassures your student sub-conscious. Arrange to meet fellow classmates in the discussion room. Talking about a subject is a great way of understanding what you have just read.

Insight – Bookworm: Make it your mission to learn how to use the library, by searching for books and accessing online resources. It will save you a lot of time and energy in the future.

▶ Classroom

If you enjoy working with others, find fellow students and have a classroom session. This is an excellent way of gathering new thoughts, perspectives and opinions. Find the right people and you will be surprised at what you can produce. One of the unconscious advantages here is that you get so wrapped up in your subject conversations it may not feel like you are actually working. That's a good thing, right?

▶ Coffee Shop

Perhaps you may like to study in the coffee shop, surrounded by real life. Not only can you have a regular dose of caffeine on demand, but the comfy chairs and informal environment could be exactly what you need. It is also a good chance to hang out with the 'ology' students.

Considerations

There are considerations that must be made when choosing a place to study. For instance, at home you can be easily distracted, which draws your attention away from the important task of studying. But by knowing this and being aware of these distractions, you can make a conscious choice to either work or not when the time comes. It takes discipline to work at home.

Just going to the library is not enough. Beware of people who say they have been slugging away in the library all day. They find it reassuring, but what have they really done? You do not have to spend ten hours in the library to make yourself feel better. If you have done quality work, then you deserve a break.

A scheduled timeout is a great way of breaking up your work period. This is called healthy procrastination and is something to look forward to. It can be an escape from the pressure of being a Zen student. It should be something you enjoy and want to do. The purpose is to release endorphins, whether you choose to laugh with your friends or sweat it out in the gym. To their detriment, most students put the 'pro' in procrastination. If you are going to do it, do it right.

Insight – The Great Escape: We found our own personal outlet was to play football or tennis to escape and let go of all challenges faced when being a student. It was a great way to socialise, get outside and raise our heart rates above 100bpm.

Study Dynamics

When we seek to discover the best in others, we somehow bring out the best in ourselves.
- WILLIAM ARTHUR WARD

Working in isolation can be liberating, you know what you have to do and you just do it. Only you can judge whether you have done enough. You can create an environment in which you are comfortable, work at your own pace and do things in your own unique way. Being a maverick is cool, we have all seen Top Gun. When working alone, you can get in the zone, lose yourself in the task and experience creative flow.

Though from our experience, a blend of both working on your own and group work will give you the best chance of success. Other people's perspective on a subject can be useful in helping you to develop your own view. Explain theories and concepts to your less clued up friends. It helps you to remember them in a meaningful way and when it comes to writing that essay or revising for that exam you can draw on those memories.

Remember the help of your allies can be invaluable but only you will know if it is a useful way of spending your time. Beware of members of your network who do not pull their weight or are a constant source of distraction, we call these people 'wasters'.

Once you have confidence in your study group, split research or readings within the group, and then present it to each other. It is an entertaining way of getting to know lots of content. Essentially you get all the information you need to know without the workload. We call this the 'people squared' theory.

Insight - Groupthink: A psychological phenomenon that occurs within groups of people. It is a mode of thinking that occurs, when the desire for harmony in a decision-making group overrides rational thought. This can lead to a bad decision being made. In context of group work at university, it can be as simple as someone explaining a concept incorrectly and nobody questioning them.

Real Life: Teamwork

```
11.05am - Lecture Building
```

Behavioural Finance. End of first lecture. Rob and Dan looked at each other. Failure on this course seemed inevitable. Maths, Theories and Formulas, it was complete information overload. Perhaps they were in over their heads. They needed the credits to get their first class degrees. It looked impossible to learn everything separately. The only solution was to work together.

A term later, it looked a lot more confusing than it actually was. They managed the workload between them, breaking everything in half. This gave them more time, they explained topics to each other and their understanding grew. Teamwork prevailed. Mission accomplished. Both attained a first on that course.

Make Notes, Not War

What are you going to do when you walk into your first lecture, merely sit there and listen? You can do this, but you are unlikely to remember everything. This is where effective note taking introduces itself. The ability to recite the key points and learning material of a lecture is integral to your success. There are plenty of aids to help you do this.

If there are lecture notes available beforehand, print them, read them and annotate them during the lecture. If notes are unavailable, take a writing pad with you and write down any key topics or concepts. Some students rush to copy down everything the lecturer says, without understanding what they are being taught. Do not just write down the lecture verbatim, you will not have time for this. Some lectures are recorded and made available to students as a podcast or tape. Listening to the lecture again can help you to retain information, it can also come in handy in case you miss a lecture.

Insight - Doodleism: An uncommon academic illness seen amongst more artistic students, who choose to annotate their notes with drawings to the detriment of their focus.

Some students may bring laptops or tablets with them. These are useful because you can instantly access course information and type notes easily. However, do not be fooled by these devices, for every useful function, there are twice as many distracting applications. Do not be lured into thinking you need this technology, it may do more harm than good, after all you are there to listen and learn from a person not a machine.

Insight - Commodity Fetishism: People experience social relations as value relations between things. In terms of the lecture, don't assume the person with the gadgets is the most intelligent.

The best way of absorbing information in lectures and classes is to get involved. This interaction helps with your understanding and pushes you to think actively, which is a great way to stop you from daydreaming. People think that just turning up to a lecture is enough, but it's not. You have to engage with the subject matter, but do not ask too many questions, nobody likes a smart arse.

Step III
- WHEN TO STUDY -

Are you a morning person or evening person? Some people like to wake up early and have their work done by the afternoon, others like to wake up late and work into the dead of the night, when nobody else is around. There are benefits to both, for example studying during the day is a common human activity but at night there are often less distractions. You need to analyse your energy levels at particular times of the day. When do you feel most awake or most tired? The key is to be aware of your own individual body clock and design your working day around it. The science behind this is known as the circadian rhythm. Find the hours that work best for you. Remember, the early bird catches the worm but no one sees the night owl.

- CONCLUDING THOUGHTS -

The 'Art of Studying' is the first chapter of this book for a reason. It is your starting point. Studying is the most important thing in your life right now. It is up to you to put yourself in the right state of mind.

The truth is those who understand how to apply the art of studying will excel. Studying is a skill you will need far beyond your degree. It is the ability to apply yourself to any task and complete it. Studying increases your ability to learn. It may be hard at times, but it will make things easier in the future. Think long term. Undoubtedly, it is easier to study something you love. So, learn to love your degree.

Studying can be viewed as both a science and a philosophy. On the one hand, if you want to succeed at university, you have to study. On the other, studying at university gives you a foundation of knowledge that will sculpt the way you interpret the world. Studying allows you to make up your own mind.

STUDY HIT LIST:

→ Establish your own system of organisation
→ Find the working environment that best suits you
→ Develop knowledge by working on your own
→ Create insight by working in a group
→ Take effective notes
→ Discover your circadian rhythm

GOOGLE ATTITUDE CHALLENGE:

Can you carry out a SWOT analysis on your approach to studying?

How to Write the Perfect Essay

Have no fear of perfection – you'll never reach it.
- SALVADOR DALI

Writing is an exploration. You start from nothing and learn as you go.
- E.L DOCTOROW

Mission: To understand the most effective way of writing a first class essay using the bricks and mortar strategy. Learn how to reverse engineer. Create an essay worth publishing, every time.

- ACADEMIC MASTERPIECE -

The process of writing an essay can be broken up into various tasks. We can guess what you are thinking, these tasks are boring. But they are not, not when you look at it from our perspective. Here is the lowdown. You have to write great essays to get a first, so you best learn to enjoy doing it. The good news is you can.

Writing can be hard, at times getting words on the page can seem like an impossible task. We are sure JK Rowling had days where nothing productive came about, but she persevered. All it takes is a slight change in perspective. Do not put limits on your work. Imagine what you are producing is a worthwhile piece of academic history. See it is an opportunity to convey your perspective on the chosen subject. You need to fall in love with the words you produce. This mindset will allow you to gain perspective and increase your knowledge of a subject without it feeling like a chore.

The Foundation

Here is our philosophy on creating a piece of work that you can be proud of, broken down into simple steps that you can identify and complete.

We found that separating an essay into two activities works best. We call it the bricks and mortar strategy. Like building a house you must have all the raw materials ready before you can begin construction, the same applies to a first class essay. The bricks are the content, this is the raw knowledge that you must demonstrate to the reader.

However, the bricks are nothing without the cement that makes them strong. This mortar is what gives your essay structure, it allows you to create an argument and best demonstrate the points you are making. It is not simply about putting bricks and mortar together. It takes a skilled workman to build a strong wall. This is where your skills will develop to create an essay that won't just blow away in the wind.

Remember the quality of materials you use will affect the quality of your outcome. Your task is to source the best material and then convey it in a captivating way that sparks the reader's imagination. So here is how to find those bricks.

- BRICKS -

Let us set the scene, it is the day your essay question is revealed. People are excited. There is anticipation in the air, and now is your opportunity to put the first class formula into practice. How should you begin?

The Question

You have to break down the question, in order to build up an answer...

The question is your starting point. It guides the direction of your research. Every essay question will contain key words that direct you in formulating an answer. Refer to any guidelines, these will help you to understand what is required. Once you understand what your question is asking, you can then grow your tree of knowledge.

Reverse Engineering
(Growing the Tree of Knowledge)

Reverse engineering is the process of exploring every aspect of your topic to discover what is relevant to your essay. Each discovery leads to the next. By doing this you will familiarise yourself with the essay topic. Done strategically, you will develop knowledge about the subject, which can translate effectively into your own work. Follow the steps below to grow your tree of knowledge.

1. The Lecture

Okay detective, go back to the lecture in question and re-read it. After all, it was put together by your lecturer and will contain the ideas that they want you to understand and demonstrate in your writing. Speak to them directly and find out what they are looking for in the essay.

Insight – Words of Wisdom: When your lecturer mentions the essay topic during a lecture, they will usually say something profound. Copy down those exact words and shoe horn them into your essay. We did this all the time, the lecturer will never remember exactly what they said, but subconsciously the words will resonate with them. Bingo, higher marks.

2. The Recommended Reading

Usually a lecture or essay question will be based on a particular reading. Read this at least twice and make extensive notes. Keep this one close, a good place is under your pillow. Understanding this will provide you with the core insight you need in order to develop a first class answer.

3. The Recommended Reading's Bibliography

This is a gold mine. To develop a robust answer with relevant research, you must explore books and articles related to the essay question. Look at the recommended reading's bibliography. After all, the author of the original reading had to develop their concepts from somewhere as well. Initially, choose articles with titles that are directly related to your topic, and then explore the others.

Insight – The Litmus Test: There is a quick way to decide whether or not an article is worth reading. Read the abstract at the start of the article and the conclusion. If there is no mention of the topic or idea that you are writing about then there is no need to carry on reading.

4. Supplementary Reading

Within your course handbook, under each lecture heading there will usually be a list of supplementary readings. Your lecturer picked these, so make them feel good by including them in your essay. By incorporating relevant supplementary readings into your essay answer, it demonstrates a willingness to explore the topic further. You may well discover a valuable insight that sets your response apart from others.

5. Other Bibliographies

Explore the bibliographies of all of the readings you find relevant to your essay topic. This will help you to branch out your tree of knowledge even further. By doing this, you are likely to find material that others will not. You may even teach your lecturer a thing or two.

Back Door Approach

Although growing your tree of knowledge is vital. To give your essay that 'je ne sais quoi', you need to produce an answer that is multi-dimensional. Below are a few simple ways of doing this.

▶ The Internet

A keyword search goes a long way. A good search can give you access to everything that is relevant on the web. Chances are you will discover a random website that offers a different way of looking at something. If you feel it is valid, incorporate this view into your own writing.

Insight – Google Books: A way of accessing books remotely online. This method is cost effective and will add depth to your bibliography. However, only selected content can be viewed.

▶ Networking

Asking around is the shrewd way of getting your fellow students' perspective on a topic. They may be able to provide you with good leads. But beware of people who 'know' what they are talking about, sometimes they don't.

▶ Other Subjects

By drawing on congruent ideas from other subjects, you are showing the reader that you are thinking creatively about the essay topic. Despite how it may sometimes seem, your degree has been designed to give you a broad and deep understanding of a particular subject. There will be cross learning between different courses. Identifying similar theories between topics could help you stand out from the crowd. It is not that difficult when you are looking. Try it.

Insight - The Wikipedia Argument: Use Wikipedia with caution. It is not an accepted method of academic research, paraphrasing sentences from the site will flag up on plagiarism checks. Our advice is to use Wikipedia to develop your understanding of a particular topic. As you know, Wiki's articles are generally easier to understand than your average academic textbook. Also, the references for each article can be useful in directing your research.

▶ Summary

The back door approach is about taking inspiration from unlikely sources, to give your essay an edge. So do not feel restricted by the above list. We have found valuable insights in quotes, news articles, films and even songs. It is funny how often you can use a film quote in your essay without it being noticed. If you are intellectually aware, they are easier to find.

Key People

Listen to many, speak to a few.
- WILLIAM SHAKESPEARE

During 'essay time' the library is a bit like the Serengeti, you see people from your course grazing. They are all hunting for key pieces of information that will enhance their essay without having to put the effort in. The first class student knows there is a better way of finding material. It is vital to identify two characters on your course. One is the 'inside man', and the other is the 'leak'.

The inside man was previously known as the teachers pet. In school, they had little use, other than their ability to soak up the teacher's attention, giving the rest of the class a break. However, now the inside man or woman is useful. This is the person who constantly talks to the lecturer. The majority of lecturers will enjoy the attention and offer advice. The great thing is this usually takes the form of an essay lead, possibly a useful journal article or even a direct tip on what to revise for an upcoming exam.

The leak is the person to avoid if you want to maintain originality in your work. They are friends with everyone on your course, including you. If you share your information with them, you are effectively sharing it with everyone. Before you know it, you will see your fellow classmates in the library referencing the exact same book or article as you. Shoot, your competitive advantage just went down the drain.

So, it is about playing the game. Your ability to leverage the benefits of knowing the inside man and the leak will help you get ahead on your course. Obviously the goal is to obtain as much key information as possible from them without giving up too much of your own research.

Insight: The Rule of Reciprocation: Robert Cialdini wrote extensively on reciprocation in his groundbreaking book 'Influence'. The rule states that people will extend you aid if you have helped them previously. Be wise and help those who may help you.

- MORTAR -

Now you have the bricks, you must cement them together. Structuring an essay is all about bringing the content to life in the most expressive and effective way. You simply need to engage the reader and convey your argument articulately, amalgamating the necessary information into the most logical and compelling prose.

Most essay questions require you to critically analyse a particular topic. This means that you have to create a line of argument, which will have developed through your research. The argument does not have to be balanced, it just needs to be supported and justified.

It is now about taking a strategic approach to answering the question. You will have a wealth of information and numerous points worth writing. However, you cannot write them all. You need to build drama into your essay, in the sense that each point must keep the reader interested and wanting more, like the season finale of your favourite television show. Here are our thoughts on the classic essay structure.

▶ Title

We think every piece of work deserves a title. It gives your essay character. It does not have to be thoughtful or quirky, but a good title frames a piece of writing. It shows the reader the value you place on your work.

▶ Introduction

The introduction needs to be easy to read, to describe what you are going to do and spark the reader's interest. That's it. So, imagine picking up a DVD and reading the synopsis on the back cover. It will either make you want to watch the film or not. That is exactly how your introduction should be written, like a seductive synopsis of your essay. Go ahead and add a bit of intrigue too, lead the reader down your rabbit hole.

Insight – LIFO: Last in, first out. Always write your final introduction at the end. Your content and structure may change throughout the writing process. This will ensure your introduction actually corresponds to what is in your work and is not just some abstract paragraph that had 'good intentions'.

▶ Main Body

Structuring the main body of your essay requires choosing content that will link together. It is no good making many different points if they are not consistent with one another, even if they all answer the question.

The main body should be divided into a succession of paragraphs. Each paragraph should contain a theme or topic, based on one aspect of your research. Each theme should be backed up by supporting statements, evidence, interpretations, examples and analysis.

At the end of every paragraph, you must briefly explain how you have answered the question. Then write a sentence that links to the next paragraph. Although these sentences use up your word count, they will make your work seamless and demonstrate your logic in answering.

When writing an essay, it is definitely about quality over quantity. It is poor practice to bore your reader with information overload. Instead try to write something that you would want to read. Pick a theme and stick to it, your work will be stronger for it. Bear in mind that you cannot say everything on a particular topic in 2000 words, so don't. Say something profound, something powerful.

Insight – The Rule of 3: A principle in writing that suggests that things that come in threes are inherently funnier, more satisfying or more effective than any other number of things. The reader is also more likely to consume information if it is written in groups of three.

▶Conclusion

Don't overcomplicate the conclusion. Summarise what you intended to say and then say how you have done it. Give your perspective on the question and what thoughts you want to leave the reader with. This should include other unexplored lines of argument. State why you think the essay question has been relevant, and finally add a killer quote. Something memorable and reflective to really hit home, perhaps even linked to your title. Do not rush the conclusion. It is the part the reader is likely to remember the most.

Insight – Court Evidence: It is hard to get an essay answer wrong, providing you support your well-structured argument with academic references.

The Critical Approach

The majority of university work requires some form of critical analysis. It is the essence of academic work. A critical approach involves not passively accepting everything you read. Take nothing at face value. Just because an author has published an article does not mean they are always right. Develop this skill by evaluating, questioning and assessing your fields of study.

If you are being asked to 'critically discuss' a theory, then you need to convey your opinion and interpretation, based on the surrounding context of the theory. The common error many make is to simply describe other academic critiques without comparing and contrasting them. Do not do that. Remember, you are being asked to be critical. You must study and evaluate the claims made by the academic experts. Summarising their opinions will not get you a first. Add your judgement to the question. Do not be descriptive, be critical.

Referencing

A vital skill for any first class student is being able to reference in true Harvard fashion. Unless you want to be diminished into the league of plagiarisers then pay strict attention to what we have to say. Referencing is simply recognising the sources of information you have used and attributing them to the author's original work. It includes anything you have read or found, be it ideas, words, concepts, theories, data or quotes.

Think of this as a kind of thank you message to the referenced source, your acknowledgement of their work. It may seem a little confusing at first, but it is really not that difficult. You just need to learn the process. Before you know it you will be referencing like a Harvard pro.

The primary reason for referencing is to avoid plagiarism, trust us, you do not want to get caught up in that web of deceit. Plagiarism is a form of intellectual theft. Unintentional or not, you will be accused of stealing another's work. It occurs when you use the words and ideas of another without citing where you got them from. To avoid this notorious academic crime, always state your source.

Now you know how important referencing is to the academic world. Be sure to look at your university guide for the rulings on referencing to fully understand what is required. Universities can vary. Check out our guide at the back of the book, The Ten Commandments of Referencing.

Insight – Reference Drop: When referencing, be careful not to simply summarise a reference. It is much better practice to state why it is relevant to the question and use it to make a point.

Finding your Voice

All the world's a stage, and all the men and women merely players.
   -   WILLIAM SHAKESPEARE

It is as Shakespeare said, life is a play and you have to be playing the right role. When it comes to penning essays, this means you have to adopt the appropriate academic writing style. Your essay must mimic an actual academic piece of writing. Though this may seem like an unnecessary hoop to jump through, this tip will repay you many times over.

Essentially you have to pretend to be a professor and write your essay accordingly. You have to act as if, well on paper at least. Not only will this role-play help you get kick-started, you will also find that you begin to use new words, big words, words that you didn't even know were in your vocabulary. The 'synonym' function in Microsoft Word is your new best friend.

Eventually your new pseudo super-genius writing style becomes natural. To begin with, study the writing style of the papers you are required to read for your course. Listen to how they sound and emulate that. Use the written word to speak to your lecturer on the right terms, even if you do not always understand what you are saying.

The truth is, this sounds like some bureaucratic baloney and it probably is. Someone somewhere along the line decided to write in this drawn out way and everybody else followed. For now, learn to like it. Here is a good quote to remind you that you needn't worry too much.

Educators take something simple and make it complicated. Communicators take something complicated and make it simple.
- JOHN C. MAXWELL

Insight – Me, Myself and I: When writing your essay, you have to decide whether you will write in the first or third person. Traditionally, in academia, it is better to give a commentary rather than make self-assertions. However, this depends on the type of course you are doing and the marking criteria for each individual piece of work.

Real Life: Exit Strategy

9:00pm - The Rectory House

1,994 words. Jake was finished. All that was left to do was the final proof read of the words that he had spent countless hours crafting. Upstairs, Dan was typing furiously. He craved the pressure of a deadline, it inspired him into action. However, working all night was only ever a short-term solution to a larger problem. The difference between the two was not when they typed their essays but in how they prepared for them. When the marks came in, Jake's methodical approach proved to be

better time and time again. It was only in the third year that Dan changed his act, and the all-nighters stopped.

Insight – Housekeeping: To complete your essay, apply some simple presentation rules. We recommend, double lined spacing, justified text, using a consistent font and inserting page numbers. These will give your academic masterpiece a polished finish.

Multiple Deadlines

It is very common to be set more than one essay at a time during term. Each one set by a different lecturer, who has no regard for your overall workload. Only when you have mastered the art of juggling deadlines are you truly on the path to becoming the Zen student.

It is always better to give all of your attention to one task at a time to ensure it is completed fully. The same strategy should be taken when writing more than one essay. It does not matter if you focus your energy on each essay a day at a time or a week at a time. Just ensure that you complete each task without leaving any loose ends.

- SLEDGEHAMMERING -

Okay, there is one more aspect to constructing that wall. We call it the sledgehammering. You need to take a sledgehammer and make sure that the wall stands up to a good smashing, otherwise known as the editing process. This is the process of making sure that your essay is coherent, articulate and effective.

Start with the basics. Check your spelling, punctuation and grammar. The best piece of advice we can give you, is to print your essay and read it aloud, slowly. You will instantly pick up on any silly mistakes you have made.

Read through your work and confirm you have addressed the question correctly. Look at each part in detail. Is your introduction concise and does it set the right tone that is consistent throughout? Check your main body, each paragraph should comprise of relevant information. Ensure there are no unnecessary sentences. Do not repeat yourself. Do not repeat yourself. Does each paragraph flow together effortlessly? The conclusion is the last thing your reader sees. Make sure it stands out.

Once you are happy with your own editing. Have somebody proof read your essay, somebody who is going to be honest and say if you are writing poorly. This provides a fresh outlook on your work. Ask them to suggest any improvements. Once you have your finished article, you are ready to go. Send it away for processing.

Insight – The Final Thesis: Not all courses require you to write a dissertation. Don't be afraid if you have to do one. It is an opportunity to write your final academic masterpiece. Apply all of the writing skills you have learned over the course of your degree. Usually you will be assigned a tutor to work alongside you. Utilise their help and apply the bricks and mortar strategy one last time.

- CONCLUDING THOUGHTS -

You are now ready to write the next academic masterpiece. Consider all we have spoken of. Apply the bricks and mortar strategy. Remember, being different sets you apart. Be creative in your writing and opinion because a thought-provoking paper will grant you much greater marks than a generic opinion. Do not be afraid to sail against the wind.

Essay by essay, your style will improve and that academic tone of writing will become second nature. Strive for excellence in every piece of work you do. This is the first class attitude. Achieving that elusive perfect essay may be unattainable, similar to the way the greyhound never catches the rabbit on the racetrack. However, keep in mind, the winning greyhound does get pretty close.

ESSAY HIT LIST:

BRICKS
→ Break down the question
→ Reverse engineer the essay topic
→ Grow your tree of knowledge
→ Exploit the back door approach
→ Locate the inside man

MORTAR
→ Structure your essay
→ Find your voice
→ Critically analyse
→ Reference as you go

SLEDGEHAMMERING
→ Complete editing process
→ Final proof read

GOOGLE ATTITUDE CHALLENGE:

Find out the origin of the word 'essay' and its meaning?

How to Ace the Exams

Diamonds are made under great pressure.
- PETER MARSHALL

The future depends on what we do in the present.
- MAHATMA GANDHI

Mission: Develop a unique method for handling exam pressure. Increase your brain capacity and find your exam ritual. Understand the differences between various exam techniques and how to use them.

- EXAM PROTOCOL -

Exams are never the most popular activity on campus. So why do we do them? More hoops. It is the system's way of testing your ability to handle pressure and recite information. For you, they are a test of character and an opportunity to show strength through adversity. With these thoughts in mind, we have developed a two phase process that will enable you to surpass the system and nail your exams.

Phase I
- PREPARATION -

The most common cause for under-performance during exam season is lack of preparation. Like any good athlete preparing for a big event, planning and practice beforehand is essential. To ensure success, you must find this discipline months before the first hurdle.

The Blind Test

The wise man knows he doesn't know. The fool doesn't know he doesn't know.
- LAO TZU

We recommend a 'blind test' for all students no matter their level of self-discipline. It is the most important task you can perform as part of your preparation. This is your starting point.

Take a notepad and a pen. Find an environment with absolutely no distractions, a clear workspace, no mobile phones, notes or books. This is your re-creation of the exam room. Choose one subject area and write everything you possibly can remember about it within twenty minutes. Once you have done this, take a five minute break. Come back and read what you have written and compare it to your course materials. List all of the essential things you missed out.

What emotion do you feel? Are you happy? Confident? Worried? Only you will truly understand the feeling, once your knowledge on a particular topic has been exposed.

The best part of the blind test is that you find out what you do not know. This highlights what you need to revise and it will help to form your study plan. Repeat the blind test as often as possible. As your knowledge grows, so will your confidence. The blind test is the closest you will get to exam conditions. Remember for this to be effective, no cheating.

Inside Knowledge

If you can find out what the hot topics are going to be on exam day, it will make life easier. We have met students that have isolated themselves throughout the exam period and achieved great results. However, it would be foolish not to spend some time speaking with the right people. Start at the source with course lecturers and teachers. Speak to them and ask questions. In our experience we have not met a lecturer that does not make a subtle attempt to direct their students down the right path to exam success.

This information will enable you to actively choose how to focus your time in order to yield the best results. The advice you receive allows you to be smart on which topics to revise. However, when strategising for each course you have to build in back-ups. It is too risky to rely solely on these leads.

Insight – Insider Trading: Some lecturers give tips because it is in their best interests. They are judged on the performance of their students. Listen out for these subtle clues but be aware of the double bluff.

Planning

It pays to plan ahead. It wasn't raining when Noah built the ark.
- THOMAS EDISON

Conducting a blind test and obtaining some inside knowledge should have stimulated your exam preparation. Now it is time to make a study plan for each course. You need to know what you don't know and know what you need to know.

Exam preparation can become a lonely place, seasoned with anxiety. In our experience many people lose direction, waste time and do not fulfil their potential. Think about how a good company will plan and strategise everything it does in its quest to maximise performance. Now it is your turn.

Rarely will you find a student who knows everything about everything. What you will quickly learn is that there is an impossible amount of content to cover in the given timeframe. On top of that, each lecturer will think that their course is the most important and set unrealistic amounts of work. Times this by the number of courses and your head may just explode.

No need to panic, there is a solution. Creating an effective study plan is the best way to achieve first class results. Avoid the casualness of a 'blowing in the wind' revision style. The key is all in the breakdown of work, your schedule of study. Separate your subjects into smaller topics and decide what you need to revise. You cannot cover everything, so prioritise.

Now you are aware of your subjects. Create a revision calendar. This involves aligning each study period of your revision to specific days over the coming weeks. Create a six to eight week plan leading up to your final exam day. The purpose is to provide you with a balanced plan of action, covering the necessary material. Sticking to this plan will be your motivation, put it up on your bedroom wall.

Futures and Options

During your degree, you may have the option of choosing complementary courses on top of the mandatory list. Be strategic in your choice. Decide what you like and evaluate how the workload for each course will affect your study plan. Check to see whether the course is exam or coursework orientated. A coursework only module will mean one less exam paper. Maximise your performance. Find your strengths and choose accordingly.

Insight – Risk Aversion: Exams by their nature incur more risks than coursework. You never know the exact details of an upcoming exam. But with great risk comes great reward. You can realistically attain

80-90% in some exams. This is far less likely in academic coursework.

Group-Board Testing

Knowledge is wealth that can be shared for free.

A few weeks into your revision, spice things up a little with group-board testing. Take a group of students and find an empty room with a whiteboard. It can be a good idea to book a room as we lost count of the number of times we were politely asked to leave.

One by one, present an exam topic to each other using only the whiteboard and a pen. There is no right way of doing this, but the key is to create an open environment of discussion, interaction and listening. From personal experience, when done properly this is the most effective technique for recalling knowledge in an exam. Unlike blind testing you are harnessing the power of many brains on to a blank canvas. However, be careful when picking people, you will soon discover who is worthy of a second date.

Insight – Study Buddies: Some people can be distracting. Work with students that are focused and have something to offer. We found a good mix of academic abilities was best. Working with people that need things explained can reinforce the concepts in your own mind.

Practice Exams

Practice is the best instructor.
- PUBLILIUS SYRUS

It may sound obvious but when preparing to do an exam, prepare by doing exams. Practice exams can be viewed as an evolution of the blind test. You are now applying your general knowledge of a subject to specific questions. Studying past exams is an integral part of preparation. It keeps your revision concentrated on central themes while practicing that exam flair. By studying the type of questions asked, you will gain a good idea of the exam structure and what is expected. Ensure you obtain the exam solutions to check your work.

Academic Celebrities

'Academic Celebrities' are the theorists that just keep appearing throughout the subjects you study. They are the experts in your field. Remember them and learn to name drop with precision. Memorise the most important things they have said including the year published. Use them in your answers to show a deeper understanding of a topic. This covert technique will make you stand out from the crowd.

First Class Cramming

First class cramming is all about condensing the necessary information into small bites that can be easily remembered during the exam. It is not about learning things for the first time, the night before the exam. At the beginning of your revision period, you should explore the whole of your subject and make notes on all of the key topics. As you become more aware of these topics and begin to remember them, your brain will need only a small trigger to recall each piece of information.

Write these triggers down to create cramming notes. You can carry these with you right up until you walk into the exam room. This way, each concept will be fresh in your mind. There are a few ways of using your cramming notes. Firstly, look at them and recite each complete piece of information, expanding on what you have written down. Secondly, test yourself to see if you remember every one of your cramming points.

Cramming is all about filling your short-term memory with the information that you need to pass the exam. The mind works by association. Allow each piece of information to associate with the next in any way you can. It can be completely abstract providing it helps you to remember the key points. If you have put in the revision time, then using triggers to recall larger chunks of information is a good exam strategy. When you are cramming, do not forget to quiz yourself to see how much information you have retained.

Insight - Cram-storm: Once the exam starts, try to write down your cramming notes as part of your brainstorm. Having your memory triggers written in front of you will make them much easier to recall during the exam.

Phase II
- TECHNIQUE -

Exam technique is an art form, practiced and then mastered by first class students. This section explores some of the different ideas that could work for you in the thick of the exam period. Ultimately, maximising success will depend on your ability to understand and apply what works best for you as an individual.

Clockwork

Always remember that you are absolutely unique. Just like everyone else.
- MARGARET MEAD

You are going to find that people work on all kinds of time zones at university. Remember the circadian rhythm we spoke of earlier. Well now we are going to take this one step further. The exam period becomes a time of sleep and revision, revision and sleep. If you want to maximise your potential you have to live, breathe and sleep your subjects.

```
Real Life: Discover Your Exam Ritual

3.00am - The Rectory House

The alarm sounds, six hours until exam room
isolation.

In a drowsy slumber, Dan hits snooze and
stumbles down to the kitchen. The jingling
sound of ice cubes hitting an empty glass
```

awakens him further. He downs a pint of
chilled water that shocks his internal
systems into motion. He follows this with
the remains of a protein rich meal from the
day before. Now it's time for a shower. Two
minutes hot, three minutes cold. He is
freezing, he shivers but now he is awake.
He feels alive.

The silence is comforting as he passes by
Jake's room. Up the stairs Rob's room is a
ripple of activity. The tapping sounds of a
keyboard traverses down the corridor.

He goes back into his bedroom and dresses.
Now it's time to begin his pre-exam ritual.
Almost six hours of brain-typing, cramming,
brain food, hydrating, stretching, short
breaks and a clear sign of insanity –
talking to himself. His ritual is finalised
with one strong cup of coffee and a fresh
walk to the examination room with Rob and
Jake, including open discussion. Now he is
ready. Now it is time to perform.

Getting up at 3am, six hours before an exam is not best practice for everyone. However, expectations of typical behaviour can be thrown out of the window during an intense exam period. It does not matter what your peers, parents or even pets think. The exam period is about finding your own rationale in a time of disarray. Develop an exam ritual that will allow you to peak at the right time.

Natural Nerves

Natural nerves are extra hormones released into your bloodstream at a time of panic or danger. Before an exam it is normal to feel nervous, even during the exam this feeling can remain. Friends and loved ones will tell you 'don't panic' and 'just relax'. This is hardly helpful when you feel your whole future is being assessed in one intensified moment.

Learning to accept these natural nerves is part of life. Anyone at the top of their field, from athletes to world leaders will still experience them. The only way to eradicate them is to stop caring, but that is not the attitude of a first class student. Recognise these nerves. Realise that the only reason you are anxious is because something important is on the line. Remember the more prepared you are, the less likely nerves will take over.

Insight – Nerves Everywhere: There is positive correlation between the amount of nerves and the importance of an event. It is visually noticeable just how much more relaxed students are outside the exam room in the first year of their degree compared to the final year.

Nuts and Bolts

You have done exams before, so you know the basics. We are not going to insult your intelligence by listing them for you again here. That is not what this book is about. However, here are a few considerations we think are valid when it comes to sitting an exam.

Remember that time is a precious commodity during an exam. It needs to be spent evenly across all available marks. One perfect answer will generate less overall marks compared to finishing all questions averagely. Budget your time for each question and stick to it.

At the beginning of an exam, always spend a few minutes brainstorming the question. This helps to unlock the different pockets of knowledge in your brain and will reduce the chance of hitting a brick wall.

If you have missed a key concept or point in one of your answers, do not worry. Simply write it down on a blank space further on and mark it with an asterisk. Use this asterisk to show the examiner where you want to include it in your answer. This keeps your work tidy.

Economics of the Exam

Every student should write non-stop until the end of the exam. It is simple economics. The more valid points you get down, the more likely you are to get marks. Minimise waffle and maximise content. It is about hitting the 'sweet spot', finding the equilibrium between quality and quantity.

Insight - Special Delivery: If you are pressed for time, include any pieces of critical information in your conclusion. You may be able to pick up extra marks. Get it down before pens down.

Post Examination Anomaly

The exam room you just walked out of two minutes ago is history. You cannot change anything. Focus on what you can change, the future. Beware of spending too much time talking to others about the exam. Accept the chatter for exactly what it is, just that.

Insight – Time and Motion: Some students predict their exam marks. If you are going to do this, then at least make it worthwhile and write them down. It can be an interesting comparison when your actual results get released. You will gain a valuable sense of your performance during exams.

Brain Food

If you are struggling to concentrate then consider eating some of our tried and tested brain foods: pumpkin seeds, broccoli, blueberries, bananas, oily fish and nuts. Don't forget to stay hydrated.

Insight – Gives you Wings: Caffeine based energy drinks and coffee are only a very short-term solution to energy and concentration levels. If you do have to use them, be sure to get the timing right. A caffeine low in the exam room is not good.

- PRESENTATIONS -

And one more thing...
- STEVE JOBS

Public speaking is apparently the biggest fear in the world. There will be times at university when you may have to give presentations. Even if you feel that you are not naturally entertaining, becoming aware of how to present well will help you immensely. You probably will not be able to choose the subject, however, you do get to choose what you say on the matter. It is always easier to talk about things that interest you. So, search for information and facts that you can deliver with conviction.

Your presentation is no different to a West End show. You must prepare and rehearse behind the scenes so the final performance is flawless. People so often ignore this aspect of the work. Giving a good presentation is not magic. If you know your material off by heart, you can concentrate fully on presenting it. You can be completely present in the moment and connect with your audience.

Here are a few practical tips to make your presentation slicker than the average:

- Understand that pausing during your presentation is not a bad thing. It may feel like forever to you, but to your audience it is hardly noticeable.
- You must deliver your presentation at a steady pace.

- Talk slowly and project your voice to the person sitting in the back of the room.
- Deliver each sentence to an individual and make eye contact with them.
- Asking questions of your audience will help you to interact with them.
- Most importantly, don't forget to smile.

You have to say what you mean and mean what you say.
- PROVERB

- CONCLUDING THOUGHTS -

The majority of people do not get excited about the prospect of exams. Nonetheless, they are inevitable. The system dictates that exams are the main way of regulating knowledge. It is your opportunity to set yourself apart from the crowd. Try to see them for what they are, a challenge, nothing more and nothing less. Yes there is a chance to fail, but there is also a chance to succeed. The techniques in this chapter work, incorporate them into your preparation. They will help you to manage the pressure of the exam period.

Your preparation and mindset are integral to exam success. Let your preparation become an obsession. Give it everything. And before you know it, they will be over. Keep in mind, the only pressure you are under is the pressure you put on yourself.

EXAM HIT LIST:

PREPARATION
- → Conduct a blind test for each subject
- → Uncover the hot exam topics
- → Create your revision plan and calendar
- → Execute group-board testing
- → Utilise practice exam papers
- → Know the academic celebrities
- → Apply first class cramming

TECHNIQUE
- → Implement your exam ritual
- → Accept natural nerves
- → Cram-storm at the start of your exam
- → Minimise waffle, maximise content
- → Optimise your exam time
- → Ignore post exam chatter

GOOGLE ATTITUDE CHALLENGE:

Which famous scientist failed their first university entrance exam?

The Lifestyle

All life is an experiment. The more experiments you make the better.
- RALPH WALDO EMERSON

A lifestyle is what you pay for; a life is what pays you.
- THOMAS J. LEONARD

Mission: After reading this chapter and putting what we say into action, people will want to be you. Discover the best place to live off campus. Learn to balance your academic genius with an intense social life effortlessly.

- YIN AND YANG -

So now you know how to learn, study and write like a student. It is the time to act like a student, the first class student.

There are many preconceptions of the student life. Some good, some bad. It is all down to perception. Students are often described as lazy, a burden on society, party heads, binge drinkers, untamed, excessive sleepers and so forth. To be honest, some of these statements are justifiable. There are those that do drink extreme amounts, go out every night and do everything but the bare minimum for their degree.

This is one way to go through university. However, there is a better way. We know you can have just as much fun as the person who simply plays without working and feel miles better for it. It is all in the balance between work and play, the essential university Yin and Yang.

The concept of Yin and Yang is an ancient Chinese notion of balance. It is the belief that there are two great opposite but complementary forces in the universe. The principle of Yin and Yang is a desire for balance between these forces, the interdependence of opposites. Work and play are your Yin and Yang right now. These are the two biggest forces at university and how you balance them will determine your success.

We imagine you have come to university to not only attain an excellent degree but also to have the time of your life. This chapter will enlighten you about achieving this balance through the benefits of people, partying and property.

Expand Your Horizons

The first thing you notice when you set foot on any university campus is diversity. You see people from all over the globe and all walks of life. This is a completely new experience in your life and it is easy to feel unsettled. However, you can turn this unease into a chance for self-development. University should be one of the greatest experiences of your life and this is where it begins. It is the place to embrace new culture and make lifetime friends.

Enter freshers' fair, the university market for sports and social clubs. Take a walk around and get a feel for what is going on. Join interesting clubs. This is a chance to do that thing you always wanted to do. If you are feeling adventurous join something completely new like the snowsports society, kickboxing club or even, the chess team.

Insight – Hard Sell: At freshers' fair, all of the clubs will be pushing the hard sell to sign you up there and then. They want cash up front because your money sets up their budget for the year. So, give some thought to the clubs you want to join and do not waste your money.

Once you have found your new array of friends, it is time to enjoy yourself. Finding fun and trustworthy friends can be one of the most valuable possessions taken from university. Jim Rohn, the business guru, once said you are an average of the five people you spend the most time with. We are not going to tell you how to choose your friends. Our advice is to learn from each other. Learn from what they do right and what they do wrong. Keep an open mind on everyone you meet. That is the key. Your friends, whoever they are, will add deeply to your university experience.

At university, your circle of friends will expand exponentially. Social networking sites have made this whole process much easier. Leverage this technology to your advantage, take names, make friends and make contacts. You never know when they may come in handy. Somewhere down the line, that programming student you met yesterday may be the key to your future success, or maybe you could be the key to theirs. Invest in yourself, build strong relationships and take risks.

The Facebook Syndrome

Beware, social networking sites such as Facebook are a double-edged sword. They can be hazardous to your mental health and extremely detrimental to your studies.

Facebook Syndrome is a deliberate or unknowing desire for the constant use of Facebook in every aspect of life. Common symptoms include:

- An excessive time spent scrolling through Facebook pages, to the extent that social activities are neglected.
- Anxiety or obsessive thinking about what is on your wall.
- Insisting on Facebook as the primary means of communication.
- Updating your status on everything you have done, doing or about to do.

It is good to utilise the benefits of online social networking. However, if you are falling victim to the Facebook Syndrome then turn off those notifications and log out.

- WORK HARD, PLAY HARD -

By working hard, you get to play hard guilt-free.
- JIM ROHN

At university, you can design your lifestyle. It is a myth to think you have to work non-stop to get a first class degree. Balance is good, Yin and Yang is necessary and you have to kick back. Parties are in abundance at university and there is no better time to do it. You are young, free and wild, one big cliché. The key is to earn that party, to earn that crazy night out. Reward yourself for hard work. It is fundamental to the first class formula.

Use an upcoming event or night out as motivation to work hard beforehand. It is a much better feeling heading out knowing that essay is nearly finished rather than thinking of starting it in the morning. This requires self-discipline, an activity that has to be practiced, the good news is, the more you practice the easier it gets.

Self-discipline is the act of controlling one's actions, desires and emotions with the intention of improving oneself. It is the essence of success. You will need to master this to reach your goals. It is a balance. After a late night out, get to class early. This will kick-start your new self-control system. Maintaining the university Yin and Yang between work and play is the key to enjoying your time at university in every respect. Do not go out to escape, go out to enjoy.

Insight – Candles: Self-discipline is not the same as burning the candle at both ends. Decide if you are being smart or reckless.

Drinking

So you have earned that night out, it is time to make it great. As previous students, we all know money, unfortunately, is not in abundance. Therefore, unless you want to accumulate as much debt as parliament, here are a few suggestions.

Pre-drinks, wherever they may be, are the most efficient place to get drunk. Find a drinking partner and split the cost of the alcohol. The fun is in calculating evenly poured measures as the night goes on.

How you spend your money when hitting the bars and clubs is down to your budget, not your bank card. Unless you are very well disciplined, do not take a bank card, take cash. You can never overspend cash. And, don't forget to save some money for the cab ride home.

Insight – Vodka Vultures: Beware of poachers. They are people who hunt for unfinished bottles of alcohol at social gatherings.

The Hangover

Unfortunately, what goes up must come down. Having a great night is important, but not at the cost of writing off the next day. One of the main causes of hangovers is dehydration. Scientifically, the best way of reducing the unwelcomed effects of alcohol is to drink plenty of water. Start the recovery process while you are still out. Instead of ordering that last Vodka and Lemonade twenty minutes before close, get yourself a glass of water. Once you get home, drink more water before going to bed. This will really flush the alcohol through your body and reduce dehydration. The next day be sure to replenish the nutrients you lost with a glass of refreshing orange juice.

There is no such thing as a hangover cure, just remedies that work for some people, like taking paracetamol, drinking coffee or going for a run to sweat it out. Find out what your best remedy is and stick to it. Do not allow hangovers to set you back.

Healthy Body

Physical fitness is not only one of the most important keys to a healthy body, it is the basis of dynamic and creative intellectual activity.
- JOHN F. KENNEDY

Staying fit and healthy can be a daunting task. If you are not careful, university can become a lethal concoction of late nights, alcohol and fatty foods. This presents health problems to students as their bodies experience changes for the worse. It may even be a shock to some students who have moved away from home and find themselves totally responsible for their own health.

There are many benefits to getting this aspect of your life right. You control your inputs and outputs. Make commitments, set goals and then exceed them. University is the perfect place to get that dream body you always wanted. Guys, you can get that Adonis physique. Girls, you can get that bikini body. There are other psychological benefits too, you will feel fresher and more attune with yourself. This is the power of exercise, use it.

We understand that everyone has different objectives and some people may not be interested in sport and exercise. After all, what is the point of being fit, if it doesn't get you good grades. However, this book is about excelling at university and we believe your body is the most powerful instrument you have. Take the necessary steps to being healthy and you will enjoy the benefits. Leading an active lifestyle will ensure your body works like clockwork. That way, when that exam period or coursework deadline comes along, your body will not be standing in the way. How do you become more productive? Richard Branson answers this one: "work out!"

Insight – Pareto's Law: A theory that states for many phenomena 80% of effects stem from just 20% of the causes. Maintaining a healthy body does not have to consume all of your time. Focus on doing the things that yield the biggest results. For an excellent understanding of this principle and how to create the body you desire. Read 'The Four Hour Body' by Timothy Ferris.

▶ Nutrition

Treat love and cooking with the same reckless abandon.
- DALAI LAMA

There is a misconception that students survive on a pot noodle diet. Food is your fuel for everything. There is no choice on this one. Eat junk food and you will feel like junk. At university, you can learn, party and work out, non-stop. Energy will be required. Neglect your insides and you will pay the price.

Food is one subject in life that is compulsory so start learning now. The Internet is full of helpful videos and information. Get yourself in the kitchen and go nuts. It does not cost much to eat healthily. Consider your shopping budget and buy accordingly. We have included some of our favourite recipes at the back of the book. They taste great and don't stretch the budget too far.

Insight – Economies of Scale: Cooking as a group is a great way of saving time and money. Remember, cook more than you need in the evening and enjoy it for lunch the next day.

Healthy Mind

Whether you think you can or you can't, you are usually right.
- HENRY FORD

Having a healthy mind is really just about having a healthy way of viewing things. By achieving the balance we have described, you are well on your way. Remember that self-pity is a waste of energy, remind yourself of everything that you are grateful of right now. Do not sweat the small things, we all know what they are, the little demons that get in the way of achieving your dreams. Inevitably you will hit bumps along the road to success, like a bad exam result. Your mistakes do not define you, what you do about them does.

Finding balance at university allows you to live completely in the present. By following our formula, you will be able to enjoy that night out, guilt free. Now is the only time that really exists. We want you to live it. It is up to you to take action.

Insight - Distractions: Leave the TVs and games consoles at your friend's house. They are an addictive waste of time. Enjoy them at your discretion. Remember the 'work for reward' mentality. Do not be consumed by these vices. There is so much variety at university, go out and see it.

▶ Relationships

Do not make someone a priority, if they only make you an option.
  - PROVERB

This section probably deserves its own book. We have seen it all, from perfect love to major break ups. Here are our thoughts on campus romance.

According to London South Bank University around a quarter of all graduates find their future partners at university. Without a doubt, being in a relationship at university can be great. The truth is you never know when love is around the corner. It is good to have someone you can 'relax' with away from studying. By setting boundaries and respecting each other's workloads there is no reason it cannot work.

The other option is single life, with no commitments or distractions. You are free to enjoy all that university has to offer, think of it as a buffet of people. By being single you avoid break-ups, which can throw you off your game.

Our advice, have no regrets, play hard to get and always act on your feelings. And don't forget to get tested.

Insight – Going the Distance: It can be hard to manage an existing relationship when beginning university. The long distance can be a major issue. It may be a challenge and you have to decide whether it is worth it.

Personal Fiscal Policy

Out of clutter, find simplicity.
- ALBERT EINSTEIN

For most students at university the lack of money can become a big problem. This section will not give you the solution to your financial difficulties. However, it attempts to point you in the right direction for managing personal funds and understanding money. Finances are quite often over complicated. Try to avoid making that emergency call to Mum or Dad for help.

Most students open a student account with their bank upon starting university. The main benefit of this is the interest free overdraft. However, you must manage the way you use this facility. Learn the concept of living within your means. Economies around the world are falling onto their knees partly because people are living beyond their means. Avoid joining the crowd here by spending five minutes at the start of each term to work out what your 'means' are.

The following equation shows you how to calculate a weekly term budget:

$$\frac{(\text{BANK BALANCE}) - (\text{KNOWN COSTS e.g. rent, bills, books, etc.})}{\text{NUMBER OF WEEKS PER TERM}}$$

Spend more than this figure each week and you will face financial difficulties sometime in the future. Stay within this figure and you will live within your means and receive the pleasure of not having to stress about money. If you find your weekly budget to be too low for your lifestyle then either spend less or get a part time job. It is that simple. Only earn what you really need. At university, your time is more precious than selling it for minimum wage.

Insight – The Borrower: Save money, borrow books. There is a common misconception that you need to buy every textbook on your course. The truth is you don't. The library is there for a reason, use it and save your funds for another venture.

- REAL ESTATE -

I am a member of a team, and I rely on the team, I defer to it and sacrifice for it, because the team, not the individual, is the ultimate champion.
- MIA HAMM

What we are about to share with you is something very abstract, yet very real at the same time. One of the biggest decisions you are going to make at university is deciding who you are going to live with. We would go so far as saying that where you live and who with, can affect the outcome of your degree. You need to put careful thought into this key decision. For most universities, it is only the second and third years that count directly towards your degree classification. Coincidentally, this is when most universities kick students off campus.

If your household works as a team then its total will be greater than the sum of its parts. This camaraderie crosses all aspects of university life. Together you will study, revise, cook, train, party and relax. If one member of the team falls behind, then it is up to the rest of you to motivate them back into action. Your household will develop its own spirit, raising the bar in all aspects of your university experience. You will be identified by your house, so what do you want it to say about you?

Real Life: The Rectorian Spirit

4.22pm - The Rectory House

The dining room. In the centre of the room, a large table overflows with commotion. A sea of papers, pens and laptops define the tone of the room. A frantic disagreement emerges between the Rectory Boys.

One gruelling question, three different answers. Who was right? The focal point of the room shifted away from the table. Objects in the room became distant as the discussion erupted. Each Rectorian attempted to justify their answer with passion and conviction.

It did not matter who was right. Between them, they would find the correct answer.

▶ Who to live with

Your best friends are always a good choice, this can lead to a happy mix between non-stop partying and create that invaluable spirit of companionship when those exams roll around.

A mixture of boys and girls. This creates a great atmosphere. However, the phrase 'don't screw the crew' springs to mind.

Your beloved boyfriend or girlfriend. This hopeless romantic scene may be the picture of perfection, however there are various pitfalls to the perfect couple living in such close proximity. Deadlines put pressure on a relationship, so does the social cost of isolating yourselves away from friends and heaven forbid the devastating break-up. We have all seen how it ended for Vince Vaughn and Jennifer Aniston.

Perhaps, random, total strangers. They could be axe-murderers. But if you are struggling to find people to live with, this is always an option. They may well turn out to be the best friends you ever make. However, you have to be able to trust each other.

Other first class formula students. There are people out there who share similar ambitions. They take their degree seriously. They have read this book and are looking for you. The best thing is they can be all of the above, best friends, opposite sex, partners or total strangers. Find them and succeed together.

It is easy to think that this decision is obvious, just pick your favourite drinking buddies and you will have a great time. However, this decision requires reflection. You will see your best 'party friends' when its time for play. If you take the right approach to networking there will be an abundance of house parties and social gatherings. The best advice we can give is to find your fellow 'first class formula' students.

Accommodation

Most universities across Britain offer accommodation to their first year and international students. If you are lucky enough to be housed on campus, that is great, enjoy it. However, the real challenge comes when you have to move off campus into privately rented accommodation. We think there are a few important things to consider when finding a place to live.

▶ The myth of the accredited housing list

This list is all hype. It comes out early merely to scare students into settling for below-par housing offered to them by cheap landlords who do not want to pay a letting agent. Although it is worth checking, there are some exceptions, for instance the nice family who have a house to let.

▶ Letting Agents

We strongly recommend using a professional. However, in our experience, half of the letting agents working around a university town are cowboys/girls because they have a cornered, ever-replenishing market. Take each one you meet with a pinch of salt. They do have a wider range of properties. Enquire early and tell them what you are looking for. Make lots of phone calls.

▶ Where to live

The obvious benefit of living as close to the lecture rooms as possible is the ability to get up late and still make it to that all important 9am class. However, some people may prefer to keep some distance from campus. Perhaps this gives them a sense of purpose when travelling to university. Depending on the distance you live from university, you will have to decide how to travel. For example are you going to walk, cycle or drive to campus? Can you afford to pay for the petrol? Do you even have a car?

On a serious note, living close to university can be great but the house you live in is important too. After all, you may well be studying there one day. Ensure that your room has enough space for a desk, wardrobe and bed. Detached houses are a noise haven, the perfect setting for house parties.

Insight - Break Clause: The academic year is shorter than a calendar year. If you are not planning on living in your house over the summer or will be changing residence, ensure that your letting contract has a six-month break clause. This allows you to end your tenancy early at no cost. Or alternatively pre-arrange a ten-month let.

Cabin Fever

Here are some basics for a pleasant home life at university. Moving in is always fun. The first team decision needs to be made, the allocation of rooms. Remember you will spend a lot of time in this room, make it a good one. It is never as simple as everyone coming to an agreement. No doubt, a lively debate will ensue. We settled the debate by creating a pricing structure for each bedroom. The highest bidder for each room wins. Natural economics take over and the best room should end up costing a premium and the smallest room should give someone rent relief. It is economic supply and demand. If that idea fails, then call shotgun.

The Negotiator

Whether it is negotiating a hundred pounds off your new rental accommodation, trying to escape paying that overdue library fine or getting a drunken mate into the club. The skill of negotiation will serve you well in life and can be practiced often throughout university. Here we have compiled a few tips that we think may enhance your deal making talent:

- Show the other person how they benefit from what you are offering. People often want to know what is in it for them so always appeal to their interests.
- Never give anything away without getting something in return. If someone is interested in your dinner, tell them they can have some, providing they do the washing up.

- State a number not a range. The other person will unquestionably choose the number which suits them. For example if you offer your old books to someone for between £50-£80, they will offer £50. Be assertive and choose a number you want.

Bear in mind that a successful negotiation is one where both parties win. Be nice. Create positive relationships wherever you go, you never know when you may negotiate with these people again. If you are really interested in negotiating skills read Donald Trump's 'The Art of the Deal'.

- CONCLUDING THOUGHTS -

Exploration is really the essence of the human spirit.
- FRANK BORMAN

This chapter has considered just a few aspects of the university lifestyle. At university, there is always something to do, somewhere to go or somebody to meet. It is a jungle of activity. You can feel lost in the new surroundings. To find your feet, consider all of the things we have talked about in this chapter. Network and meet new people. Learn to understand the human body. Work hard, play hard and enjoy guilt free gratification.

However, do not stop here. It is impossible to tell you everything about lifestyle in this short section. Go forth and explore. Ultimately, it is what you make it. Go out and experience for yourself the Yin and Yang of university life. All we can do is teach from our experience, we cannot teach experience.

GOOGLE ATTITUDE CHALLENGE:

Is hot or cold exposure better for burning body fat?

The Winning Mentality

Strength does not come from winning. Your struggles develop your strengths. When you go through hardships and decide not to surrender, that is strength.
- ARNOLD SCHWARTZENEGGER

Winning is not a sometime thing; it's an all time thing. You don't win once in a while, you don't do things right once in a while, you do them right all the time. Winning is habit. Unfortunately, so is losing.
- VINCE LOMBARDI

Mission: Discover what motivates you and use it to put the first class formula into action. Understand how to recognise opportunities, deal with failure and become a leader.

- THE HEART OF A CHAMPION -

In previous chapters we have spoken of the necessary steps required to be the best. This chapter is about developing the vital all-conquering attitude, the heart of a champion.

Remember university is a journey, a marathon. Therefore it requires a marathon mentality. This is not an undertaking that will be over in a day, a week or a month. This adventure will last for at least three years. Essentially you must develop the right attitude from day one. But what is the right attitude? It is a combination of ideas, discipline and drive. These ideas are present throughout this book. Every little thing we have discussed is an aspect of this winning mentality.

Keep Your Eyes on the Prize

Every morning in Africa, a gazelle wakes up. It knows it must move faster than the lion or it won't survive. Every morning, a lion wakes up, and it knows it must move faster than the slowest gazelle or it will starve. It doesn't matter if you're the lion or the gazelle. When the sun comes up, you'd better be moving.
- MAURICE GREENE

Stay focused on your goals and do not allow any small problems to hold you back. Small problems can be anything from a bad essay mark, an argument, to being strapped for cash. It boils down to having motivation in the face of adversity. Motivation is going to be the fuel to your fire. By reading this book you know you have a desire to be the best. Now is the time to find the motivation to put the first class formula into action.

To begin, you have to find out why you want this, who are you trying to impress? Who are you challenging? Is this for you or someone else? By answering these questions honestly, you will find your motivation. Have no doubt about it, there will come a time when you feel discouraged. This is when you need to reflect on why you are doing this and what you are trying to achieve. This provides you with the foundation to carry on.

The reasons for obtaining your degree will evolve as you study, therefore so will your motivations. In your quest for a first class degree you will require constant sources of motivation to maintain your high focus. Motivation can be found everywhere. It can come from within, from your surroundings or from other people.

Writing goals and hit lists are great for keeping you focused. Monitoring your performance through short-term objectives will illustrate your progression. These small goals will give you focus, allowing you to concentrate on the things that are truly important to your success. Keep a quote, an inspirational picture or poster on your wall. A little thing like this will push you on when you need it.

Rising Up from the Fall

Our greatest glory is not in never falling, but in rising every time we fall.
- CONFUCIUS

The toughest but integral part of success is dealing with failure. It is only with failure we learn how to succeed. The inventor, Thomas Edison, failed thousands of times before he succeeded in creating the light bulb. He famously said "I have not failed. I've just found 10,000 ways that won't work". Take from this his enthusiasm in the face of failure. After all, there may come a time when you work very hard for a piece of coursework or an exam and get results far below those you expected. An outcome like this is a test for you, you are either going to rise or fall. You have a choice.

If you fail, take a step back and work out where you went wrong. This process allows you to establish rational reasons for your poor result. Developing this awareness means you can do better in the future. Many say failure is the best teacher, so if you do make a mistake, learn from it, do not waste it. It is your attitude to failure that will ultimately determine your level of success.

Do not fall victim to the self-pity paradox. This is the idea that, by not trying your best or leaving something to the last minute you have a justifiable excuse for failure. This is what losers do. They subconsciously decide not to give a task their full attention and upon discovering they have failed will say the following: "Oh well I did leave it to the last minute" or "I knew I should have spent more time on that". This reassurance feels better than knowing they tried hard and failed, because this way they never test their true ability. This is a self-defeating attitude and will not get you anywhere. Face the music and see what you are made of.

We all have the capability to do great work. However, the process of discovering this ability is not always easy. Failure may be necessary, it can guide us to do something in a more effective way. It can draw out our potential and our ability to adapt. Do not let the fear of failure prevent you from being your best.

Real Life: Learning from Failure

1.00pm - The Rectory House

Second year, first term. It was an average afternoon in the Rectory house. Jake was practicing a new trick, Dan was cooking and Rob was working out. The essay results were in. Excitement. Jake had the department on the phone. They found out their results. Jake: 70, Dan: 71. The phone is passed to Rob, 48, he asks again to make sure. Jake and Dan look at Rob, he does not want to say his mark. 48, a third class essay. Not a good start for an aspiring first class student, a big disappointment. Rob goes back upstairs to reflect on his result.

Besides the initial shock, Rob feels like a loser. He has failed this essay. He sits there in disappointment dwelling on his result thinking about what to do next. He decides this is a defining moment. He vows never to let this happen again. He found out why he obtained such a poor result and moved forward positively.

The Brand You

We are what we repeatedly do. Excellence, therefore, is not an act but a habit.
- ARISTOTLE

Treat yourself as a brand of success. Imagine what that represents. What it takes. This is what you are. Taking the first class approach in everything you do will undoubtedly lead to your success.

Think about what a brand is, what it symbolizes. If we say Nike, you probably picture Michael Jordan, Roger Federer or Lance Armstrong in other words world-class record breaking athletes. Think BMW, Mercedes or Audi and high-quality German car manufacturers come to mind. Now consider all we have spoken about and conceive what you think a first class student would personify. This student would embody a whole host of positive traits. Hard working, organised and sociable to name a few. All you have to do is live this brand, it is that simple. Live and breathe this attitude. If you find yourself in a challenging situation, ask yourself what would a first class student do?

Chains of habit are too light to be felt until they are too heavy to be broken.
- WARREN BUFFET

Warren Buffet, the famous investor, has often spoken about the importance of learning to incorporate positive traits into your personality. To find these qualities he suggests a scenario where you choose to receive 10% of the future earnings of five of your classmates. He says that you would do this based on how you perceive them to be, it is a qualitative assessment. Use this exercise to identify the good attributes of those around you and integrate them into your personality. It is an excellent way to develop your character. The quickest way to change yourself is to hang out with people who already are the way you want to be.

Your personality and behaviour will be your brand, make it a great one. The way you perceive yourself is the way you will be perceived by others. Live up to the brand you portray. Keep yourself motivated, inspire others and always do your best. You will succeed.

- CONCLUDING THOUGHTS -

The winning mentality is the key ingredient for the first class formula. It exists in all of us. Without it, all the tips and tricks in this book do not mean a thing. Act as if you are the first class student and you will become the first class student. Don't think, just do.

GOOGLE ATTITUDE CHALLENGE:

Who has missed the game winning shot 26 times?

The Last Chapter

Success is a journey, not a destination. The doing is often more important than the outcome.
- ARTHUR ASHE

In this book, we intended to show you that obtaining a first class degree and having a great time at university are not mutually exclusive. We know you can do both. Every insight in this book shows that it is possible with the right attitude. Hard work is necessary but so is having fun. University is what you make of it. That is the experience.

It is time to become the Zen student. Everything you do at university is part of this journey. We can guide you but we cannot hold your hand. Go out and use the first class formula. Recognise that you set your own limits and decide what you are capable of. Prove that you can achieve what you set out to do. If you can do that, then you can do anything. Now you know what is possible, how are you going to make it happen?

Bonus Material

The Ten Commandments of Referencing

1) As soon as you begin writing your essay, create a bibliography on the final page or on a separate document.

2) Reference your material as you go along and it will not become a burden. List each new reference in your bibliography. Never leave it to the last minute. Looking for references you found two weeks ago is not much fun.

3) Replicate the referencing style set by academic publications and keep it consistent throughout.

4) *Under review* for plagiarism. Please skip to number 5.

5) If you are utilising an author's argument to support your own line of argument but are not directly using their words then it is acceptable to insert the author's surname and year of publish in brackets at the end of the relevant point in the text.

   For example:
   To truly be radical, consumers need to regain their identity as engaged citizens in democracy (Gabriel and Lang 2006).

6) It is also possible to use an author's argument to counter a point in your writing, this is useful for developing a balanced line of argument.

For example:
Instead Bell (2008) suggests that films can represent unreality, which potentially disrupts an audience's view of these phenomena in everyday life, such unrealities could be the dystopian futures depicted in science-fiction films.

Similarly, Cote and Pybus (2007) argue that part of the current population's capacity to live is extended through the particularities of their subjective socially networked relations.

7) Sometimes it is helpful to use an author's exact words because they directly support your argument and it would be sacrilege to articulate their profound wisdom in your own words.

For example:
"Texts that one person may judge realistic another may not, depending largely on life experience or situated cultures" (Hassard and Holliday 1998, p.2).

8) Thou shalt use Harvard referencing.

9) Read:

Pears, R. and Shields, G. (2010) *Cite them right: The essential referencing guide.* Palgrave Study Skills: London.

10) If you are still unsure, go back to 1) and repeat.

Recipes

Mama's Special Spaghetti Bolognaise

Originating from the Northern Italian city of Bologna, spaghetti bolognaise is a classic dish for any continental kitchen. Harness this recipe, test your skills, experiment with flavours and create your own special spaghetti bolognaise. Remember to save any leftovers, this tastes great the following day.

You need:

500g of mince beef

1 chopped onion

1 can of peeled tomatoes

50g of tomato puree

4 sliced button mushrooms

Pinch of oregano

1 crushed garlic clove

Salt and pepper

Olive oil

Wholemeal spaghetti

Parmesan cheese

Equipment:

Frying pan

Pot

Chef's knife

Chopping board

Colander

Instructions:

1) Heat pan, add a drizzle of olive oil and fry the chopped onion on a medium heat for a few minutes.

2) Add the mince beef to the pan, season with salt and pepper. Mix and break up the mince until it is browned.

3) Boil the spaghetti in a pot of salted water for 10 minutes.

4) Drain any excess fat out of the pan containing the mince.

5) Add the oregano, sliced mushrooms and crushed garlic to the pan.

6) Mix in the tomato puree and the can of tomatoes to make the bolognaise.

7) Drain the pasta and serve onto plates, top with bolognaise. Sprinkle with grated Parmesan.

8) Fini.

Danny California's Power Chicken Stir Fry

Danny California's power meal is the perfect dish after a long day of studying, writing or exercise. Conjured up after months of testing on muscle beach, this recipe provides all the necessary nutrients for a quick recovery. A swift and easy method makes this dish great for those short on time.

You need:

2-3 sliced chicken breasts

200g wholemeal egg noodles

200g beansprouts

Sliced red or green peppers

1 chopped broccoli floret

1 chopped onion

Soy sauce

Olive oil

Salt and pepper

1 crushed red chilli (optional)

1 beaten egg (optional)

Equipment:

Large frying pan or wok

Chef's knife

Chopping board

Instructions:

1) Heat the frying pan, drizzle with olive oil and throw the chicken in. Cook on a high heat until the chicken is white.

2) Season with salt and pepper.

3) Throw the peppers, onion, broccoli and chilli into pan. Stir continuously.

4) Add the egg, beansprouts and egg noodles.

5) Continue stirring.

6) Add a splash of soy sauce for flavour.

7) Serve onto plates.

8) Fini.

Fernando's Sizzling Fajitas

An authentic Tex-Mex recipe originally created by the Texan cowboys and Mexican pancheros of the 1930's. Add some international flair to your diet with this tasty meal. A great one to share with friends.

You need:

3 sliced chicken breasts

6-8 flour tortillas

1 chopped onion

2-3 chopped peppers

Garlic seasoning

Fajitas mix

Olive oil

Sour crème (optional)

Guacamole (optional)

Low-fat natural yoghurt (optional)

Cheddar cheese (optional)

Salsa (optional)

Equipment:

Large frying pan or wok

Chef's knife

Chopping board

Instructions:

1) Heat the pan, drizzle with olive oil and throw in the chopped onion.

2) Add the sliced chicken and cook on a medium to high heat until it is white.

3) Add the chopped peppers.

4) Sprinkle on the fajita mix and stir.

5) Microwave each tortilla for around 10-20 seconds.

6) Once the pain is sizzling, take it off the hob and place on the table (on a kitchen towel, do not burn the table).

7) Lay a tortilla on your plate. Add either yoghurt, sour crème or guacamole to your wrap. Followed by a serving from the frying pan.

8) Sprinkle with grated cheese, add salsa and fold your wrap.

9) Fini.

Recommended Reading

The 4 Hour Work Week by Timothy Ferriss

This book tells you how to escape the 9 – 5, live anywhere and join the new rich. It will affect the way you view the world.

How to Win Friends and Influence People by Dale Carnegie

The most successful self-help book of all time. It is easy to read and provides simple rules for communicating effectively with anyone.

The Richest Man in Babylon by George S. Clason

An inspirational guide to personal money problems which presents eleven ancient Babylonian tales revealing the way to financial success.

Rich Dad, Poor Dad by Robert Kiyosaki

A ground-breaking book that describes the lack of financial education taught in schools. It provides a unique economic perspective for creating wealth and keeping it.

The Alchemist by Paul Coehlo

A beautiful story, that describes the journey of a young man out to discover his destiny.

Influence by Robert Cialdini

The classic book on persuasion. It explains the psychology of why people say yes and how to apply these understandings. It describes the six universal principles of persuasion, how to use them and how to defend yourself against them

The Magic of Thinking Big by David J. Schwartz

David Schwartz proves that you do not need to be an intellectual or have innate talent to attain great success and satisfaction - but you do need to learn and understand the habit of thinking and behaving in ways that will get you there.

The 4 Hour Body by Timothy Ferriss

An uncommon guide to rapid fat loss, incredible sex and becoming superhuman. Based on more than a decade of research, the collective wisdom of hundreds of athletes and medical doctors, as well as thousands of hours of jaw dropping experimentation.

The Art of the Deal by Donald Trump

An overview of a week in the entrepreneur's life, opinions on everything from football to New York mayors. Stories of Trump's best real estate deals and a discussion of the deal maker's art.

The Game by Neil Strauss

A highly entertaining exposé of a fascinating secret society, the world of the pickup artist. An insight in to human behavior. True or false, decide for yourself.

Tuesdays with Morrie by Mitch Albom

This true story about the love between a spiritual mentor and his pupil has soared to the bestseller list for many reasons. It reminds us of the affection and gratitude that many of us still feel for the significant mentors of our past.

Do it Tomorrow by Mark Forster

A complete system that will enable almost anyone to complete one day's work in one day.

Glossary

Academic Celebrity: Any person(s) that have contributed significantly to a particular field of study. They are experts and their names are constantly appearing on your course.

Academic Crime: The act of using someone else's academic work to your own advantage without referencing and crediting the source.

Academic System: The current rules and regulation in place that students have to abide by in order to acquire their degree. For example, attending lectures, writing coursework and sitting examinations.

Accredited Housing List: A student housing list that is released before the end of term, including potential rental properties around the university area.

Amalgamate: To combine or unite to form one organization or structure.

Bibliographies: A list of the books referred to in a scholarly work, usually printed as an appendix.

Brand You: It is the process of thinking about yourself as a brand. Recognising that how others perceive you is based on your personality and performances.

Bureaucratic Hoops: Unnecessary and overcomplicated administrative procedures. Conditions that a student has to meet, in order to be successful.

Camaraderie: Mutual trust and friendship among people who spend a lot of time together.

Circadian Rhythm: The body clock of a human being, in line with the Earth's rotation. Recurring naturally on a twenty-four-hour cycle, even in the absence of light fluctuations.

Creative Flow: Entering an independent state of creativity.

Exam Ritual: A series of actions or type of behaviour regularly and invariably followed by someone immediately prior to an examination.

Exponentially: Increasing and expanding more and more rapidly.

Face value: To accept someone or something just as it appears; to believe that the way things appear is the way they really are.

First Class Formula: The Art of Studying + How to Write the Perfect Essay + How to Ace the Exams + The Lifestyle + The Winning Mentality = The First Class Formula.

Freshers' Fair: An event held at the beginning of the academic year during which a variety of events are held to welcome new students.

Group-Board Testing: Is an exam preparation technique used by a group of students. Each one takes turn to present a topic using only a whiteboard and a pen.

Harvard Referencing: The most common and widely accepted form of referencing personal work. Also known as author/date referencing.

Healthy Procrastination: Scheduling a timeout or delay in order to break up your work period.

Hit Lists: A short list of things to accomplish.

Intellectual Theft: Beyond the parameters of an 'Academic Crime'. Using someone's intellectual property (intangible assets such as music, literary, artistic works, words, phrases and discoveries) in your work without referencing and giving credit to the source.

Je ne sais quoi: An indefinable quality.

Maverick: An unorthodox or independent minded person.

Means (living within): In financial terms, only spending equal to or less than the money and resources you have rather than borrowing money to fuel a lifestyle that is unsustainable.

Means to an End: Something that you do because it will help you achieve something else.

Mind Palace: It is the act of relying on memorised associations in the brain to remember content and/or information.

Natural Nerves: Anxiety and nervousness felt by a person when about to do something of importance, in a moment they have to deliver. Extra hormones are released into the bloodstream at this time of panic.

Networking: Finding a new group of people to exchange information, contacts, and experience for professional or social purposes.

Noise Haven: A place of safety or refuge where noise does not have to be limited.

Paraphrasing: A rewording of something written or spoken by someone else.

People Squared Theory: The principle that a group of people can yield a much larger workload than an individual.

Plagiarism: The practice of taking someone else's work or ideas and passing them off as one's own.

Pro in Procrastination: A common behaviour amongst students of delaying or postponing an action or task by finding other unimportant things to do.

Proof Reading: The final checking of a piece of work for errors and mistakes, done by another person.

Prose: Written or spoken language in its ordinary form, without metrical structure.

Pseudo Super-Genius: Not genuine but exceptionally intellectual.

Reverse Engineering: The process of taking something apart or breaking it down to analyse its parts and workings in detail.

Self-Pity Paradox: The contradictory act of self-absorbed thinking and unhappiness over ones own troubles.

Shoe Horning: Simply, putting something in.

Shotgun Rule: Calling shotgun is the act of claiming a position for oneself.

Student Subconscious: Regarding the part of a students mind, which is not fully aware but which influences actions and feelings.

The Blind Test: An exam preparation technique used by an individual student. It involves creating an exam room like environment and testing ones knowledge of a particular topic using only pen and paper.

The Inside Man: The student on a course that is always talking to the lecturer or teacher. Usually the Inside Man will gain invaluable information.

The Leak: The student on a course that is friends with almost everyone and is very open with information.

The System: A student's personal organisation of studying that seeks to yield the greatest results.

Trade-off: A situation that involves losing one quality or aspect of something in return for gaining another quality or aspect.

Tree of Knowledge: The expansion of knowledge through books, journal articles and other readings using bibliographies.

Verbatim: In exactly the same words as were originally used.

Waffle: When writing, showing the reader a failure to make up ones mind by saying the same things over and over.

Wasters: A person(s) that spends most of their time procrastinating, distracting others and fails to get much work done.

Yin and Yang: The belief that there are two great opposite but complementary forces in the universe.

Zen Student: The Zen student balances their studies with their social life. They know that the journey is just as important as the destination.

A Message From the Authors

Thank you for reading this book. We wrote the first class formula solely for the experience you will have when obtaining your degree. What you do after graduation is up to you. We wish you every success. If this book has helped you in any way, we would love to hear from you, please tell us your story at:

stories@firstclassformula.com

Acknowledgements

This book would not have been possible without the help and valuable contributions from the following people. Thank you to Jamie Hall, Tracy Lorraine Law, Kim Pompilii and Carol Banfield. We would not have written this book if it were not for the support given to us by our family and friends. Of course we cannot forget the people that made our university experience what it was. Ladies first, thank you Nadine, Penelope, Becca, Bora, Laura, Joy, Jackie, Amy, Sabrina, Julia, Siobhan, Hannah, Holly, Zoe, Sheila, Raquel, Vanessa, Maria, Maggie, Meera, Rhoda, Natalie, Tanya, Sophie, Hannah, Loren, Zara, Veronica, Vic, SK, Katie, Danielle, Daniella, Sarah-Jane, Linn, Keeley, Lisa, Amanda, and Sarah. Gentlemen, thank you Adrian, Lowley, Reggie, Tom, Gowers, Señor, Mike, Lynchy, Josh, John, Dave, Kieron, Pat, Nate, Rob, Seyi, Steve, Chiz, Charlie, Dillamore, Nunn, Khalid, Mark, Sarwar, Umair, Eriz, Jackson, Lavs, Giles, Gordie, Toby, Rich, Towey, Sunny, Phil, Adere, Rayner, Thom, Tim, Alex, Grimesy, Wes, Jack, Vassili, Spiros, Lambros, Tsis, Jordan and all of those who came in and out of lives throughout university. A final thank you to our lecturers Chris, Hitch, Steffen, Tom, Khalid, Magda, Andrew, Ceri and Kat.

NOTES

NOTES

NOTES

NOTES

NOTES

NOTES

NOTES

NOTES

NOTES

Printed in Great Britain
by Amazon.co.uk, Ltd.,
Marston Gate.